GREATER
LOVE

Books in the Woman's Workshop Series

Behold Your God: Studies on the Attributes of God
    by Myrna Alexander

Designed by God: Studies on Healing and Wholeness
    by Kirkie Morrissey

Faith: Studies on Living the Christian Life by Martha Hook

Forgiveness by Kirkie Morrissey

The Fruit of the Spirit: Studies on Galatians 5:22–23
    by Sandi Swanson

Greater Love: Studies on Friendship by Jean Shaw

*Growing Godly: Studies on Bible Women by Diane
    Brummel Bloem*

Heart Trouble: Studies on Christian Character by Barbara Bush

Loving and Obeying God: Studies on 1 Samuel
    by Myrna Alexander

Mastering Motherhood by Barbara Bush

Open Up Your Life: Studies on Christian Hospitality
    by Latayne C. Scott

Perfect In His Eyes: Studies on Self-Esteem
    by Kay Marshall Strom

Talking With God: Studies on Prayer by Glaphré

Time, Talent, Things: Studies on Christian Stewardship
    by Latayne C. Scott

Woman's Workshop Series

GREATER LOVE

STUDIES ON FRIENDSHIP

JEAN SHAW

Lamplighter Books Grand Rapids, Michigan
Zondervan Publishing House

To the women of
Westminster Reformed Presbyterian Church

"Friendship is the inexpressible comfort of feeling safe with a person having neither to weigh thoughts nor measure words."   —George Eliot

CONTENTS

INTRODUCTION

"A friend is someone who knows what you're really like, and loves you just the same."

There is a person to treasure! Perhaps you have never had a close friend. Perhaps you had one, and she moved away, or died. Your life is a jigsaw puzzle with a missing piece.

You may be a person with a lot of acquaintances, but no one special friend with whom you can share your thoughts and dreams. You are not lonely—there is always someone around willing to go shopping or to the movies. In fact, the groupiness of your lifestyle is a mixed blessing. It would be wonderful to know one person really well—one person whose relationship to you didn't depend on a planned activity. Sitting under a tree would be fine if she sat there, too.

Are you involved in a friendship that is stagnating? You both seem to talk about the same things everytime you get together. How can you add some variety? You feel yourself

9

being dragged down, exploited, even led into sin. How can you get out?

No problem? Friendship for you has been rewarding. You'd like to have more friends! You see friendship as a potential force for spiritual growth, evangelism, discipleship, building up the body of Christ. On a less lofty, but equally important level, friends are fun!

It may be that none of these descriptions fits you at all. You enjoy studying the Bible, and if the Bible has something to say about friendship, you're eager to dig in.

Whatever has prompted you to commit yourself to this workshop, be assured that God's Word has much to say about friendship. The Old Testament gives some classic examples. Christ Himself considered the subject very important. Paul's friends meant so much to him that he names them in his letters.

Above and beyond human relationships is the divine friendship of Christ, our Creator, Savior, and Lord. Can you truthfully exclaim, "What a Friend I Have in Jesus!"? This workshop will introduce you to this incomparable Friend, and help you to find other friends as well. "Two are better than one," says Ecclesiastes. Come and see.

1

WHAT IS A FRIEND?

"A friend is someone who walks in when others walk out."
—Walter Winchell

1. Write down your definition of the word *friend*. _____

   Someone who loves you for
   who you are and inspite of
   your faults.

2. Think of some friends you have had. What was there about
   them that made them special? _____

   accepting
   fun, easy to be around
   serious & light moments

_____

_____

_____

3. Think of yourself as a friend to others. What signs of friendship distinguish you? _____

   Consistent

   Genuine

   Faithful

   _____

   _____

4. What is the value of friendship?
   a. _companionship_

   _____

   b. _prayer partner_

   _____

   c. _someone to serve_

   _____

   d. _____

   _____

   e. _____

   _____

   In the Bible, David and Jonathan exemplify the highest form of human friendship. Turn to 1 Samuel.

5. Who was Jonathan? (13:16; 14:1) _____

   Saul's son

   _____

What could he expect his future role to be? _____

king

_____

Who was David? (16:1; 13) _____

Jesse's son + new king

_____

What could he expect his future role to be? _____

king

_____

6. What qualities of friendship did Jonathan display in each of the following incidents?

   a. 18:1–4. _true love + giving of himself, unselfish_

   b. 19:1–7. _spoke well of David_

   c. 20:1–23. _do anything for him, protect him_

   d. 20:24–42. _prayed together, grieved over David's situation, covered up for David_

   e. 23:15–18. _encouraged him in the Lord_

Jonathan was a giver. His name means "Jehovah has given." He reached out to find David's need, and then met it. He used his friendship with David to help David and not himself. His goal was not to *have* a friend, but to *be* a friend.

The word *friend* has an interesting history. It comes from an Old English word, *freo,* which means "free, not in bondage, noble, glad." To this was incorporated the word *freon,* meaning "to love." This evolved into *fre(o)und,* one who combines freedom with love.

7. How did Jonathan and David practice freedom in their relationship? _____

being a friend and not wanting the friendship for yourself

SHARE

How can friends practice freedom in their relationship today? _____

not keeping a clutch on your friends

Give an example of how a friend enabled you to grow spiritually, emotionally, or intellectually. _____

by seeking counsel from me, trusting me

Have you ever helped someone else to grow? How?

encouraging & praying for them

What can parents do to help their children enjoy friendships? *teach loyalty, be an example*

PRAYER

On a 3 x 5 card, write down one thing you learned in this Bible study today. Thank God for it! If you have a special need, bring it before the group. Join in prayer for each other.

CARE

Write down one need expressed by someone else. Pray for that need during the next week.

PREPARE

Read Psalm 139. What does this psalm tell you about your relationship to God? What does it say about your relationship to yourself?

2

THE PERFECT FRIEND

"Greater love has no man than this, that one lay down his life for his friends."   —Jesus (John 15:13)

The friendship of Jonathan and David may inspire us to develop such a relationship as theirs, as well it should. Oh, to have a friend so selfless! We must admit, however, that no person can be a perfect friend. No person can be with us wherever we go. For perfection and constancy, we must look to Jesus. His credentials are unexcelled.

Read Psalm 139.
1. Jesus knows us.
    a. How long has Jesus known us? (v. 16) _____

from eternity

_____

_____

b. What does He know about us now? (vv. 1–6)

(1) _(our every move)_
sitting

(2) _rise up_

(3) _my thoughts + understands_
them

(4) _plans we have_

(5) _our words before we_
say them

c. What do verses 13–15 inform us of Jesus' knowledge?
He knows every part of us

d. Jesus knows something else about us. See Psalm 44:20–21; Acts 1:24. _the secrets of_
our heart

Jesus knows our body, mind, and heart.

2. What is this person like, whom Jesus knows?
   a. Body: 1 Corinthians 15:42–44. _Corrupt,_
   dies, natural, weak

   b. Mind: Psalm 94:11; 1 Corinthians 3:18–20. _____
   vain; foolish; crafty;
   worldly

   c. Heart: Jeremiah 17:9; Mark 7:21–23. _deceitful,_
   desperately wicked, evil things

There is nothing about us to admire. A person who knew us that well wouldn't want to be our friend. She would turn away, sick and disgusted. Not Jesus. In spite of what we are, He accepts us; and what is more remarkable, He loves us.

Read Romans 5:6–11.
3. Jesus proved His love for us. What did He do? _____
   died for us while we were
   sinners; He became what
   we are

Why did He have to do this? _it was the_
   only way for us to be
   reconciled

We are so wicked, we deserve God's wrath and punishment. We should die and go to hell. Jesus took our punishment on Himself. He died in our place. When we believe that Jesus saves us from our deserved punishment, we have His promise that when we die, our souls shall live and go to heaven.

4. Jesus died for us. He did something else, also. Read John 14:16–17. *gives us the Comforter, the Holy Spirit; a friend; He didn't leave us alone.*

What does the Holy Spirit do for us? Read Romans 5:5. *gives us love for others because He loves thru us*

The Holy Spirit enables us to love others unselfishly. This same Holy Spirit enabled Jonathan to love David. What we cannot do in our own strength, we can do in the power of the Holy Spirit.

5. All of us have personality traits which are irritating. How can we discover what these are, and change them?

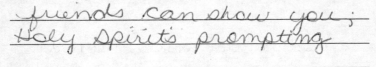

friends can show you; Holy Spirit's prompting

Today's lesson is summed up in the hymn, "I've Found a Friend." Sing it now, reflecting on Jesus, who created us, knows us, loves us, and died for us. He will always be our friend.

SHARE

Describe a situation in which you were able to love an unlovely person. This could be a child with stomach flu, an aged person with a terminal disease, a co-worker with an unpleasant personality. _____

Obnoxious neighbor boy

How did you manage to cope? *to see his future in Jesus*

What practical steps did you take to feel loving and to be loving? *Speak kindly, allow him over when I really didn't want him there*

PRAYER

Praise God for sending Jesus to die for our sins. Praise Jesus for being our best friend. Praise the Holy Spirit for helping us to be a friend to others. Petition God for any in the group who have special needs. Were any prayers answered after last week's meeting?

CARE

Using the list of names handed out today, send a card or a brief note to the person whose name follows yours. Include a verse of Scripture which has been helpful to you.

PREPARE

Read about Jesus and His friends in the following passages. What do they show us about Jesus as a friend?
  Mark 3:13–19
  Luke 10:38–42
  John 11:1–44
  John 12:1–8

Colleen 1859 Cecily Dr.

I'VE FOUND A FRIEND

J. G. SMALL

GEO. C. STEBBINS

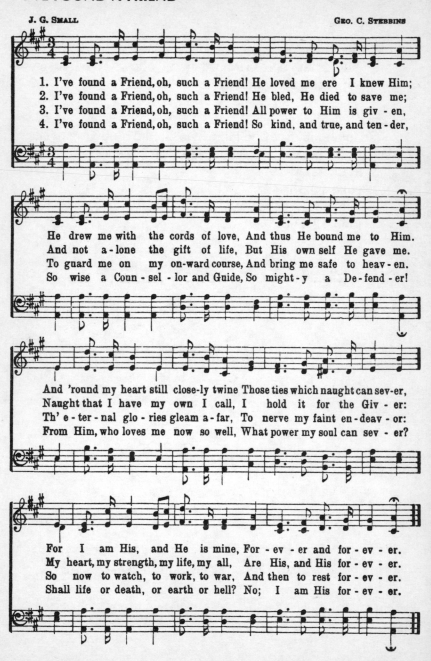

1. I've found a Friend, oh, such a Friend! He loved me ere I knew Him;
2. I've found a Friend, oh, such a Friend! He bled, He died to save me;
3. I've found a Friend, oh, such a Friend! All power to Him is giv - en,
4. I've found a Friend, oh, such a Friend! So kind, and true, and ten - der,

He drew me with the cords of love, And thus He bound me to Him.
And not a - lone the gift of life, But His own self He gave me.
To guard me on my on-ward course, And bring me safe to heav - en.
So wise a Coun - sel - lor and Guide, So might - y a De - fend - er!

And 'round my heart still close-ly twine Those ties which naught can sev-er,
Naught that I have my own I call, I hold it for the Giv - er:
Th' e - ter - nal glo - ries gleam a - far, To nerve my faint en - deav - or:
From Him, who loves me now so well, What power my soul can sev - er?

For I am His, and He is mine, For - ev - er and for - ev - er.
My heart, my strength, my life, my all, Are His, and His for - ev - er.
So now to watch, to work, to war, And then to rest for - ev - er.
Shall life or death, or earth or hell? No; I am His for - ev - er.

3

JESUS DEMONSTRATES FRIENDSHIP

"I no longer call you servants, because a servant does not know his master's business. Instead, I have called you friends, for everything that I have learned from my Father I have made known to you." —Jesus (John 15:15)

What kind of friend was Jesus?

1. Women were among Jesus' friends. Read Luke 8:1–3; 10:38–39.
   a. What had Jesus done for them? _healed_ _them_ _____

   b. What were they doing for Jesus? _hosting Him, learning from Him, serving with what they had_

c. Answer these same questions on the basis of Matthew 27:55. _He was dying for them_ _and they were ministering_ _to Him. They were there_ _"to the end."_

2. Jesus enjoyed several friendships at the same time. He loved all the Disciples, but at different intensities. Read Matthew 17:1–2; John 21:20–21.

   What disciples were especially close? _Peter,_ _James, John_

3. Jesus rendered service to His friends. In each of the following situations, what did He do?
   a. Lazarus (John 11:38–44). _raised him_

   b. Disciples (John 13:1–5). _washed their_ _feet_

   c. Disciples (John 17:6–9). _prayed for them._

   d. Peter (Matthew 8:14–15). _healed his_ _mother-in-law_

e. Mary (John 2:1–10). _made wine_
at the wedding

f. Disciples (John 21:4–6). _caused them_
to catch fish

4. Jesus accepted His friends' service to Him. Read John 19:25–27. What did John do? _took care_
of Jesus' mother

Review question 1.

5. Jesus shared His thoughts and the secrets of His religious experience "that they might be with Him." In each of the following situations, what was the subject He shared?
a. Matthew 24:1–3. _Ressurection_
distruction of the temple

b. Mark 14:22–26. _Communion,_
tangible way to remember
ressurection ; joyful song afterwards

c. Luke 11:1–4. _how to pray_

d. John 14:1–4. _He was going to_
prepare a place in
heaven for us

e. John 17:6-8. _His word_

A summary is found in John 17:6-8. _all things_

6. Jesus was patient and forgiving. What incidents give an example of these qualities?
   a. Matthew 20:20-28. _when James & John's mother asked for her boys to sit beside Jesus_

   b. Matthew 26:56. _when His disciples betrayed Him_

   c. Mark 4:35-39. _Calmed the storm at sea_

   d. Mark 9:33-35. _Cared they were arguing_

e. John 21:15–19. _asked Peter_
if he loved Him

7. Jesus accepted His friends where they were, but He had a vision of what they could become. What was His expectation in each of the following situations?
    a. Matthew 4:19. _fisher of men_

    b. Matthew 10:1 _power to heal._

8. Jesus trusted His friends. What did He ask them to do?
    a. Mark 11:1–2. _bring the donkey_
    for Jesus to ride on

    b. Mark 14:13–16. _find the_
    room for last supper

9. Jesus prayed for His friends. Read John 17:6–19. What did He pray in their behalf? _keep them,_

unify them, joy, keep from evil, sanctify them.

10. Jesus made His friends better than what they were. He influenced them by His example and conversation. You can see His influence by reading Acts; 1 and 2 Peter; 1, 2, and 3 John.

SHARE

A friend knows her friend's business. How broad and how narrow should self-revelation be? In the space below, write down what you think your friend should know about you.

_____

_____

_____

_____

_____

What areas of life would you prefer not to share? _____

_____

_____

_____

_____

PRAYER

If you have a friend with whom you can share your deepest feelings, praise God for her now. Pray for her, remembering those specific needs she has shared with you. If you do not have a special friend, ask the Lord for one. Pray for openness to the kind of friend God sends.

CARE

Is there someone with whom you have been impatient or unforgiving? Make it a specific task this week, to speak to that person and restore the relationship. Render a service to one of your friends this week.

4

THE TRAITS OF FRIENDSHIP

"Without distinction, without calculation, without procrastination, love. Lavish it upon the poor, where it is very easy: especially upon the rich, who often need it most: most of all upon your enemies, where it is very difficult, and for whom perhaps we each do the least of all." —Henry Drummond

1. Paul says that love is the most excellent way. Read 1 Corinthians 12:27–31 and list the other ways (gifts) that are excellent, but not the most excellent.

   a. _apostles_   e. _healing_
   b. _prophets_   f. _helps_
   c. _teachers_   g. _gov't – administrators_
   d. _miracles_   h. _tongues_

   These are important gifts. We have them by God's appointment. And yet, Paul tells us he is going to show us "the

OT love
"hesed"
unfailing love
Prov. 19:22

includes
kindness
faithfulness

30

most excellent way," which is love. Why is love the most excellent? _w/o it - all the others are weaghless - that's how others know we are His disciples_

2. Read Colossians 3:12–14. Paul tells us how we are to be dressed. Notice that it is love which binds all the virtues together. The Greek word for "binds" which Paul uses refers to a belt or girdle. This was the most essential part of the costume: It held all the other parts together. It was used for tucking in the skirt when vigorous activity had to be done. In cold weather it kept the tunic close to the body for warmth. It even contained slits which were used like pockets for holding tools or personal items. While a belt could be decorative, it was primarily necessary if a person was to function.

3. Read 1 Corinthians 13:1–3. Rewrite the passage in your own words, from your own vantage point. For example: "If I am the most efficient secretary in the office, but . . ." or "If I attend every one of my son's Little League baseball games, but . . ." _If I get all my expected work done & have not love, no one will be happy about it anyway because I will have turned everyone away._

_____

_____

_____

_____

_____

4. The characteristics of Love: 1 Corinthians 13:4–7. This passage is so familiar, we may be unmoved by its depth. Understanding the Greek meanings for some of the words can be helpful. As you reflect upon the characteristics of love, rate yourself. On a scale from 10 (very loving) to 1 (not loving at all) write a number in the box provided.

a. "Is patient, kind." Love does not merely endure, but takes positive action. There are people who have borne another person's ill feelings for years, but have never done anything to love that person who doesn't love them. This verse also applies to situations when we are teaching a child, or a child-like person. In addition to patience as they practice over and over, there must be help and encouragement. ☒

b. "Does not envy, does not boast." The Greek word for "envy" is related to the Greek word *zeo* "to boil," indicating the degree to which we can hate someone for being or having something we want. Love does not begrudge another's possessions, but would add to it if possible. ⑩

c. "Is not proud." The Greek word here means being puffed out like a pair of bellows. Love is free from conceit, not ego-centered. ⑩

d. "Is not rude, is not self-seeking." Rudeness is primarily selfishness. Love seeks the other person's good and happiness. One's own desires are forgotten. ⑨

e. "Is not easily angered." Love is not sensitive or "touchy," but it can be angered eventually. Our response is to be free of irritation or sharpness of spirit. See Acts 15:39; 17:16; Hebrews 10:24.   ☐

f. "Keeps no record of wrongs." The key word here is *logos*—"ledger" or "notebook." Love doesn't have to "settle the account." Love doesn't cultivate a good memory for wrongs and slights.   ☐

g. "Always protects." From *stege,* a roof. Love covers, keeps something off which threatens. See 1 Peter 4:8. Love is equal to any emergency, never giving up.   ☐

h. "Always trusts." Love believes and builds on that belief. It is not gullible, however, but has faith in people.   ☐

i. "Always hopes." Love expects growth. Something better is to come.   ☐

j. "Always perseveres." Love bears with everything. The Greek word means "like a soldier."   ☐

5. Read 1 Corinthians 13:8. What will happen to the other gifts? _Cease + pass away._

_____

_____

6. These are very high standards for love. We do not naturally feel this way. Turn back to lesson 2 and review what we are really like. How can we become this loving?   p.18

    There are at least six things we can do. Divide into six groups (if there are enough of you) and explore Scripture to find the answers. Then summarize in a few words or phrases the main point.

a. John 13:34–35; 15:9–24; Leviticus 19:18, 34; Romans 13:8–10. _Love others as Jesus_ _loved us ; be obedient to His command to love others_

b. John 15:12–13; 1 John 3:16. _lay down life for brothers_

c. 2 Peter 1:3; Ephesians 3:16–19; John 14:15–17.

d. 2 Peter 1:4; 1 Peter 2:2–3; 1 Timothy 6:3–5; Acts 20:32.

e. Ephesians 4:15–16; Philippians 2:1–4; 2 Corinthians 2:5–8; Romans 15:1–6.

f. Philippians 1:9; Proverbs 28:13–14; Hebrews 4:14–16; James 5:13–16; 1 John 5:13–15.

SHARE

Discuss the answers to question 6.

PRAYER

In silent prayer, confess before the Lord any unloving feelings that you are harboring—toward your present family, relatives, neighbors, friends, people in the church, people at work. Ask that God will give you a loving spirit. Pray for a way to make this evident to the one you haven't loved.

CARE

Do something kind this week for a person toward whom you have had unloving feelings.

PREPARE

Read 1 John 3. What guidelines for love does John give here?

5

HOW FRIENDSHIP BEHAVES

"Friendship hath the skill and observance of the best physician, the diligence and vigilance of the best nurse, and the tenderness and patience of the best mother."

—Lord Clarendon

Will Rogers said he never met a man he didn't like. "To like" is defined as "to take pleasure in, find agreeable or congenial to one's taste, to regard with favor or have a kindly feeling for." I may like people who enjoy gardening or wear purple. I like the woman at the checkout counter who packs my groceries so carefully.

To love involves warm personal attachment and deep affection. There is concern for the person's well-being. While I like all the members of my garden club, I do not have a deep affection for all of them. Some of them I only know by their name tags. I do not know if the checker at the supermarket has a happy marriage, is in good health, or has all her bills paid. I have never asked her about her well-being, nor do I think she would appreciate my probing for personal details.

It is easy to like someone. There is hardly any cost at all. To love someone is an entirely different matter.

Read 1 John 3.
1. a. According to 1 John 3:16, how do we know what love is? _____

_____

_____

 b. What should we do? _____

_____

_____

_____

2. We will probably never be asked to die, literally, for a friend.
 a. In what ways can we "lay down our lives" while we are living?
 v. 17. _____

_____

_____

 v. 18. _____

_____

_____

 b. What actions would give evidence of our love?

_____

_____

_____

3. Read 1 John 3:18.
   a. What does "in truth" mean? See 1 John 5:6. _____

   _____

   _____

   _____

   b. How would loving someone "in truth" or "in Christ" or "in the Spirit" be different from loving them not "in truth"? _____

   _____

   _____

   _____

   _____

   c. What things might we as Christians say and do that non-Christians would not? _____

   _____

   _____

   _____

   _____

4. Read the following passages. What bearing does each have on friendship?
   a. Romans 14:7, 13. _____

   _____

   _____

   b. 2 Corinthians 5:14–17. _____

   _____

   _____

c. 1 Corinthians 6:18–20. _____

_____

_____

d. 1 Thessalonians 5:10–11. _____

_____

_____

SHARE

Respond to each of the following situations. Perhaps the group would like to divide into pairs and act out the situation.

1. Leslie majored in drama in college. She loves plays and often attends performances with her friend, Mavis. Leslie is a Christian, but Mavis is not. None of Leslie's Christian friends are interested in the theater, while Mavis shares Leslie's knowledge of American playwrights. Should Leslie continue this relationship? How can she witness for Christ to Mavis? Have you ever had an interest that no one in your church shared?

2. JoAnne and Nancy always stopped in at the Frontier Lounge after work on Friday night for a couple of drinks. They had fun talking with the people there. Now JoAnne is a Christian, and she feels uncomfortable in the lounge. How can she maintain her friendship with Nancy? What purpose do bars and lounges serve? Can the church fulfill these same needs in a more wholesome way?

3. Jenny and Ruth have been close friends for years. They both attend the same church and work together on the same committees. They are totally compatible and make a good team. Neither of them has found any other friend so helpful and supportive. Should they plan to do less together and seek out other friends?

4. Marion has never learned to drive a car. She depends upon Judy to drive her everywhere. Judy loves Marion, but she is getting weary of taking her places, even though Marion always pays her fairly. What should she do?

PRAYER

Praise God for your friends, Christian and non-Christian. Ask God for wisdom in these relationships. Ask God for sensitivity to their needs. Pray for yourself, that you may be open to them helping you.

CARE

Ask God to give you one new friend this week, and then act upon his leading.

PREPARE

Read Titus 2. What characteristics does Paul give for Christian men, for Christian women, and for Christians in general?

6

THE VALUE OF A GOOD FRIEND—PART 1

"I never ask God, or hardly ever, for outward things. I do not know that I ever asked Him for glory or honor, and I hope I never shall; and I very seldom ask Him for material things apart from the kingdom; but I sometimes say things like this, that if God will give me three or four good friends, I think I can manage to the end, because love is the machinery of life and the motive power." —Randel Harris

A. ENCOURAGEMENT

While we may always think of encouragement as a positive action, it can have a definitely negative influence, if it leads to harmful or sinful action. A person may be encouraged to try heroin, for example, or to join a cult or to commit adultery. What kind of encouragement should a Christian give? And accept? We, too, can be misled.

Read Titus 2.

1. In this chapter, Paul talks about encouragement as given through teaching in the church. What is our principal guideline? (v. 1) *sound doctrine*

2. What accompanies this encouragement to change our behavior? *responsibility to teach others*

3. What is the ultimate goal of such encouragement? *behavior becoming holiness*

4. Paul specifically mentions women in chapter 2.
   a. What standards does he set for older women? *holy, not false accusers, not given to much wine, teachers of good things*
   b. For younger women? *sober, love husband, children, keeper of home, good, obedient to husband*

   c. How do you think such teaching would be accepted in your church today? Would the older women like to be taught by men? Would the younger women like to be "trained"? *generally people should look up to the older & wiser, but often they are too self-sufficient*

d. At what age do you think a "younger" woman becomes "older"? *when she is "mature"*

5. God-pleasing encouragement has certain characteristics.
   a. 2 Thessalonians 2:16 (Jesus' example.) *love, everlasting consolation*
   b. 2 Timothy 4:2. *reprove, rebuke, exhort w/ longsuffering + doctrine*

While we consider the deeper implications of encouragement, there is still a great need for such simple expressions as "I hope you continue to arrange the church flowers. They are always beautiful," or "I really respect you for staying on your diet." A few words can mean so much, but often we say nothing.

B. COUNSEL

There is a big difference between encouragement and flattery (excessive or insincere praise). A true friend wants us to be like Christ, which means she may have to disagree with us at times, or tell us something about ourselves that we find hard to accept.

Read Proverbs 27.
1. a. What are the profuse "kisses" of an enemy? (v. 6)

deceitful

b. What are the faithful "wounds" of a friend? _____

correction _____

_____

_____

_____

2. What heals the wounds? (v. 9) _____

hearty counsel _____

_____

_____

_____

3. We must have a special relationship with a friend before we can offer her counsel. Paul mentions friends in many of his letters. From the following passages, make a list of qualities which marked his close friends.

a. Romans 16:2. _helper_ _____

_____

_____

b. Romans 16:8. _beloved_ _____

_____

_____

c. 1 Corinthians 16:18. _refreshed_ _____

_____

_____

d. 2 Corinthians 13:10b. _edification_ _____

_____

e. Philippians 4:14. _helped where he needed it_

f. Philemon 22. _lodging_

Would you accept these qualities as guidelines to determine those friends from whom you would receive counsel? _yes_

Would you add anything? _faithfulness_

4. The writer of Hebrews gives helpful guidelines for counsel. Read Hebrews 10:24–25.
   a. The goals of counsel (v. 24). _good works_

   b. The means of counsel (v. 25a). _fellowship at assembling_

   c. The attitude of counsel (v. 25b). _exhorting_

SHARE

Recall some good advice that made a difference in your life. Describe the person who gave it.

_____

_____

_____

PRAYER

Praise God for His friendship. Thank Him for His encouragement and counsel as found in His word and through His people.

CARE

Perhaps you tried to help someone, and were rejected, or someone tried to help you, and you resented it. If you have been part of a damaged relationship, make reconciliation a particular aim for this week.

Think of a friend who faithfully performs some task. Send her a card or note expressing your appreciation.

PREPARE

Two more reasons why we value a good friend are her help and her prayers. Choose one of the four Gospels and read it through quickly, noting the chapter headings. Write down all the different ways that Jesus helped people. In one particular case, when He was asked to help two of His friends, He refused. Why did He say "no"?

7

THE VALUE OF A GOOD FRIEND—PART 2

"The need for friends is imperative. It is not good for man to be friendless. He was made to give and to receive, to help and be helped, to encourage and to be encouraged—to feel a bond with others. Standing alone can never satisfy. His nature requires a tie to faithful others. We call it friendship."
—Leroy Brownlow

In the last lesson, we learned about encouragement and counsel. Today we explore two more qualities which we value in a good friend: help and prayer.

A. HELP

1. When we study the life of Jesus, we see that He was not some sort of eastern mystic, sitting on a remote mountainside, dispensing advice. Jesus lived and worked with people, responding to their needs. From your reading this past week, compile a list of the ways He helped others.

_____

_____

_____

_____

_____

_____

2. How did this work affect Him?
   a. Matthew 9:36. _____

   _____

   _____

   b. Matthew 14:23; Luke 5:16. _____

   _____

   _____

   c. Luke 4:42. _____

   _____

   _____

   d. Luke 7:22. _____

   _____

   _____

3. When we help someone else, how will we be affected?

   _____

   _____

   _____

4. Paul describes many ways in which he was helped by his
   friends. Read the following passages and describe the help
   given.

a. 2 Corinthians 1:10–11. _____

_____

_____

b. 2 Corinthians 9:1–5. _____

_____

_____

c. Philippians 2:25–30. _____

_____

_____

d. 2 Timothy 1:16–18. _____

_____

_____

5. The Bible affirms that two are better than one. Read Ecclesiastes 4:9–12 for the reasons why.

a. _____

b. _____

c. _____

d. _____

A beautiful illustration of this passage is offered by single women sharing an apartment.

6. There was once a young woman who became engaged to a man who lived on the other side of town. Nightly he trudged through the wintry air, always arriving with his coat collar turned up, his nose blue from the cold. With a compassionate heart and nimble fingers, she knitted him a red wool scarf. She presented the gift one evening, expecting much appreciation. Her beloved stood there,

speechless, finally confessing that he never wore scarves, he was allergic to wool, and he didn't like red!

a. How do we decide what kind of help a person needs?

_____

_____

_____

_____

b. Is there ever a time when it is best not to help someone? Read Matthew 20:20–28. _____

_____

_____

_____

c. What should be the goal of helpfulness? _____

_____

_____

B. PRAYER

Christian friends regularly pray for each other. Paul had many friends who prayed for him, as he prayed for them.

1. Read aloud one of the following passages, noting what Paul prayed for and what he asked prayer for.

a. Romans 15:30–33.

Paul prayed for _____

Paul asked prayer for _____

b. 2 Corinthians 13:7–9; 1:11.

Paul prayed for _____

Paul asked prayer for _____

c. Ephesians 1:16–19; 6:18–20.

Paul prayed for _____

Paul asked prayer for _____

d. Philippians 1:3–6; 4:6.

Paul prayed for _____

Paul asked prayer for _____

e. Colossians 1:3; 4:2–4.

Paul prayed for _____

Paul asked prayer for _____

f. 1 Thessalonians 1:2, 3; 5:17–18, 25.

Paul prayed for _____

Paul asked prayer for _____

g. 2 Thessalonians 1:3; 3:1–2.

Paul prayed for _____

Paul asked prayer for _____

h. 2 Timothy 1:3, 18.

Paul prayed for _____

_____

i. Philemon 4–6, 22.

Paul prayed for _____

Paul asked prayer for _____

2. As we encourage, counsel, help, and pray for our friends, we are agents in the process of wounding and healing the wound. (Refer back to Proverbs 27:9.) What is an important aspect of healing? Read 2 Corinthians 1:3–4.

_____

_____

SHARE

How should we respond to praise and criticism? _____

_____

_____

_____

_____

Is one as difficult to accept as the other? _____

_____

PRAYER

Thank Christ for interceding for you before the Father. Ask Him to make you a faithful intercessor for others.

CARE

Do you have a prayer partner? Make it an objective this week to find someone who will pray regularly for you and pray for your special needs when you ask her to. Promise this friend that you will do the same for her.

PREPARE

Read 2 Corinthians 6:14–18. Beginning with verse 14, Paul gives five contrasts. Discover them.

8

CHOOSING A FRIEND

"I count myself in nothing so happy as in a soul remembering my good friends." —Shakespeare

We become like our friends. Either they will make us more like Christ, or less. Paul reminds us of this in 1 Corinthians 15:33. Write the verse here. *Be not deceived; evil communications corrupt good manners.*

There are five questions God wants me to ask about a friend.
1. Is she a fool? (Proverbs 13:20)
   a. What is a fool?
   Psalm 14:1. *says there is no God, corrupt, does abominable works*

Proverbs 1:7. _despise wisdom_
& instruction

Proverbs 18:2. _no desire to_
learn, only his heart
to discover itself

Proverbs 28:26. _trusteth in_
own heart

b. How can she cause me harm? _a companion_
of fools shall be
destroyed Pr. 13:20

2. Is she a glutton? (Proverbs 28:7)? _riotous (glutton)_
a. What is a glutton?
Philippians 3:18–19. _whose God_
is their belly (all
sensual indulgences)

glory
in our
shame

1 Peter 4:3–4. _lusts, drunkers_

Amos 6:4–6. _selfish – lavish_
upon themselves all
good things

b. How can she cause me harm? _Cause_
me to be self-centered
as herself

3. Is she leading me away from God? _a friend is someone_
who leads you in the
a. What is God's warning? (2 Corinthians 6:14–18) _right direction_
stay away - be not
yoked together with them

b. What are the signs of a dangerous friend? Read Ephesians 5:3. _fornication, all_
uncleanness, covetousness

5:4. _filthiness, foolish talk,_
jesting (course joking)

5:6. _vain words_

5:17. _unwise_

5:18. _drunk_

Proverbs 22:24–25. _make no friend_ _a/ angry, lest you learn_ _his ways_

c. How can she cause me harm? _make_ _me become like her_

4. Is she a gossip?
   a. What is a gossip? _Telling_ _confidential business_ _about someone else_   _ear pollution_

b. Does the Bible describe this as a serious sin? Read Leviticus 19:16. Who is speaking? _yes,_ _the Lord_

What is the occasion? (Leviticus 27:34) _commandments_

What is the source of gossip? (Luke 6:45) _good_ _heart or bad hearts_

When we gossip, what are we really doing? (James 4:11–12) _judging others_

c. How can a gossip cause me harm? (Proverbs 16:28; 20:19) _strife, separates friends,_ _flattereth w/ lips_

destruction/sharing detrimental info w/ those not part of the problem or solution

5. Is she upsetting God's priorities for me?
   a. Summarize God's priorities. (Titus 2:4–5) _teach younger women,
   sober, love husbands,
   love children, discreet,
   chaste, keepers at home,
   good obedient to husbands,
   that did not blasphemed_

   b. Remember what Jesus said. (Matthew 22:37, 39) _love God 1st + neighbor
   as thyself_

   c. How can she cause me harm? _to turn away from
   these priorities_

   Guidelines for discontinuing a friendship will be given in the next chapter.

SHARE

How can you remain friendly with someone who is a harmful influence? _be a higher
model of Christ and
seek to draw them to
Christly living_

What activities can you share? _____

_____

_____

_____

PRAYER

Praise God for your friends who have guided you to be more like Christ. Ask God for wisdom in all your relationships. Pray for those you know who are not Christians. Pray for Christian friends who have grown cold to biblical values.

CARE

Reflect on any past friendships that ended because you felt they would make you less like Christ. Is there some point of contact you could make that would show you still care, but would not make you vulnerable to bad influence? Christian counsel may be essential at this point.

PREPARE

Read Colossians 4:2–6 and write down the three main points.

Turn back to lesson 6 and review the value of a good friend. What kind of friend are you?

prayer to speak for Christ
walk in wisdom

speech full of grace
w/ answers

9

MAKING FRIENDS

"Even though radically different from each other, two persons may enjoy the closest friendship for a lifetime; for it is not a requisite of friendship that the participants be alike in all things: it is enough that they be alike at the points where their personalities touch. Harmony is likeness at points of contact, and friendship is likeness where hearts merge."

—A. W. Tozer

ENDING A FRIENDSHIP, MAKING A NEW ONE

If I have a friend who is causing me harm, I must draw away. And yet I do not want to alienate that person from Jesus Christ. What can I do? Colossians 4:2–6 offers some help. What are the three main points of the passage?

1. *continue in prayer*

2. _speak the mystery of Christ_

3. _walk in wisdom + redeem the time_

Here is an acrostic which may help you.

Pray for her and for myself.
Explain my position.
Act out of love.
Continue to be kind.
Enlist the help of Christian friends.

It may be a fact that no one needs to be lonely, but meeting someone—and beginning a new friendship—is sometimes the hardest thing in the world. Moving into a new community where you don't know anyone, or moving into an apartment house where the tenants prefer privacy, can leave you feeling as if no one cares whether you live or die. Soon you decide you aren't worth much anyway, so why should anyone care?

How do you find a friend? How do you find a good friend who will enrich your life even as you enrich hers? Work out the following situations in small groups.

1. Arbutus Abercrombie is a woman, just like yourself, who has recently moved into your community. She doesn't know anyone here. What are some different ways in which she can meet people as potential friends?

2. Arbutus meets a woman who tells her, in casual conversation, that she collects samovars. What can Arbutus do to extend this contact into another meeting? _Russian teakettles_

Once the seed of friendship has been planted, care must be given to keep it growing. It must have good soil (love), regular watering (respect), and fertilizer (desire for growth).

A. LOVE

Some years ago, love was described by the phrase, "never having to say you're sorry." This is a fanciful notion indeed! All of us will occasionally hurt the person we love. We are imperfect creatures even with the best of intentions. When we have offended, the most loving thing we can do is admit it, confess it, and try to rectify the wrong. What does the Bible say that love is?

1. Matthew 5:41–42. *go the extra mile; share*

2. Romans 12:9. *no hypocrisy. unmasked, good + not evil)*

3. 1 Corinthians 13:4–7. *patient, kind, not vain, not easily provoked, beareth all, believeth all*

4. Colossians 3:12–14. *mercy, kindness, forgiving*

B. RESPECT

Friendship is not possessive. I let my friend have other friends. I want my friend to be herself, not a copy of me. She has a right to privacy, both in thoughts and activities. I let her share herself with me to the degree she wishes. I neither probe, nor ask other people. What does the Bible say about respect?

1. Romans 12:10. _honor_

2. Romans 12:15. _rejoice with + weep with_

3. Romans 15:7. _receive others as Christ received us_

4. Galatians 5:26. _don't envy_

C. DESIRE FOR GROWTH

A living friendship is characterized by each friend growing spiritually, mentally, and emotionally. Unless there is growth, a friendship stagnates and eventually dies. Have you ever paid a visit to someone and found yourselves rehashing the same old stuff you talked about the last time you were together? (Marriage can suffer from the same problem.) Sharing books, magazine articles, newspaper clippings, cartoons, taking short trips together, attending a seminar, learning to make children's clothes or picture frames, or co-chairing a committee at chuch are all ways of enlivening and improving a friendship. What does the Bible say about growth?

1. Proverbs 27:17. _sharpening another_

2. Romans 5:12. _sin is contagious_

3. 1 Corinthians 8:13. _does not offend_

4. 1 Corinthians 13:5. _seeks not her own_

5. Hebrews 10:24. _"sharpen" one another to good works_

SHARE

Read the following quotation:

"When we survey, now, this initial demand of every worthy friendship for integrity, breadth, and depth of personality, we cannot fail to see that at every point it carries with it the imperative duty of growth. There may be in any relation a short-sighted sacrifice that defeats itself. One fears sometimes that mothers, for example, so give themselves to their children as to forbid all growth for themselves; and that only means, that the time hastens on apace when, with the growth of the children, the mothers will not have the self to give that then is needed. If you would not cut yourself off from later service of your friend, you must grow with his growth."

—Henry Churchill King
The Laws of Friendship Human and Divine
(Macmillan, 1937)

1. Do you think that growth is an "imperative duty"?

   It will stimulate the relationship, but can't always be the main ingredient.

2. Can we give too much of ourselves to our children?

   Probably but many don't give enough so I would say the opposite is more likely.

3. What can we do to be friends with our children when they become adults? *Share interests, listen on a respectful level, always be there for them, never give up*

4. How can we grow with our friend's growth? *See her interests and growths and encourage and exhort*

PRAYER

Praise God for those who reached out to you when you were lonely. Ask Him to help you to be sensitive to others. Ask God to make you be a friend who is loving, respectful, and desirous for growth.

CARE

Think of a friend who has a special interest. Find something in a magazine or newspaper that relates to that interest and give it to her.

PREPARE

Read the following passages and note attitudes that can destroy a friendship: 1 Samuel 16:21–23; 1 Samuel 18; 1 Samuel 19:1.

You can make more friends in 2 months by being interested in others, than in 2 years trying to make others interested in you.

To a New Friend

God knew that I was all alone,
  Strange in a strange new land.
Knew there was none to share my load,
  To care and understand;
He knew the road was rough and steep,
  That helping hands were few;
He knew my heart, and all its needs—
  And so He sent me you.

He sent me you. Your way was new
  And long and lonesome too,
So you could understand my need
  And I was kin to you.
God knew each load would weigh but half
  If it were shared by two;
He knew the strength of fellowship,
  And so He sent me you.

Together now we journey on,
  Together praise and pray,
Together love and laugh and lift,
  Together seek His way.
Now holds the road so lonely once
  A glory sweet and new,
For Jesus closer drew Himself
  The day He sent me you!

                    —Margaret Clarkson
                    Rivers Among the Rocks
                    (Moody Press)

10

SAVING A FRIENDSHIP

"If I take offence easily, if I am content to continue in a cool unfriendliness, though friendship be possible, then I know nothing of Calvary love." —Amy Carmichael

Friendship can end for many reasons. The friends may move apart—physically, mentally, spiritually. There is no longer a purpose for the friendship. Friends may separate because one is harmful to the other. When we become Christians, our values change. Those who would tempt us to love what is displeasing to the Lord have to be moved out of our inner circle.

Another way to end a friendship is by displaying a bad attitude. Friends can be getting along very well until one of them behaves in a way so unloving that continuing the relationship is impossible. Offense without correction can destroy the friendship altogether. We have an example of this in the account of Saul and David.

A FRIENDSHIP DESTROYED

We read in 1 Samuel 16:21 that "Saul liked David very much," and in verse 22 Saul says to Jesse, David's father, "Allow David to remain in my service, for I am pleased with him."

This relationship deteriorated to the point where Saul tried to kill David.

1. What attitudes did Saul have which destroyed their friendship? Look at 1 Samuel for the answers.

   a. 16:21–23. *loved him, David refreshed him w/ his harp* *selfish; using him for own benefit;*

   b. 18:2. *held him against his will; possessiveness*

   c. 18:6–9. *jealousy*

   d. 18:10–11. *tried to kill David; threats*

   e. 18:12–13. *Saul was afraid of David*

   f. 18:14–30. *afraid of David, tried to betray him*

   g. 19:1. *planned to kill David; hatred.*

2. What is the opposite, positive attitude for each negative?

   a. *unselfish*

   b. *freedom*

   c. *glad for one another's wealth*

d. _self-control, meekness_

e. _delighted w/presence ; communicate_

f. _honesty, trust_

g. _love_

SAVING A FRIENDSHIP

When a friendship is about to break up, what can we do? Jesus gives us guidelines in Matthew 5:21–24.

1. Realize the seriousness of an unloving attitude. What does Jesus compare it to? _murder_

2. Act without delay. What other activity should we put off until we have straightened the matter out? _anger, name calling ; gifts to the Lord_

3. Take the initiative and responsibility. Who is the offender in Jesus' example? _the one who got angry_

4. Aim for reconciliation. *Reconcile* means "to repair, to make good again." The common expression, "patching up a friendship," is not what Jesus means. Each party is to make concessions and create a new, and better relationship.

Love is to motivate us and dominate all our proceedings. In 1 John 4:11 we read, "Dear friends, since God so loved us, we also ought to love one another." Turn back to lesson 2 and review what kind of people God loves. No one has offended us the way we have offended God, and yet God loves us. It will help us to love others, if we keep this in mind.

WHEN FRIENDS AREN'T RECONCILED

Suppose our friend cannot love us. Her heart remains unforgiving. We may have to see her every day at work, or in church, or continue to live next door to her, feeling her hatred. What should we do?

1. Review 1 Corinthians 13:4–7. Love is described as—

a. _longsuffering_ i. _thinking no evil_
b. _kind_ j. _doesn't rejoice in iniquity_
c. _doesn't envy_ k. _rejoices in truth_
d. _not vain_ l. _bears all things_
e. _not puffed up_ m. _believes all things_
f. _doesn't behave unseemly_ n. _hopes all things_
g. _" seek her own_ o. _endures all things_
h. _" provoke easily_

2. Check these attributes of love in a situation where the other person does not love back. Which of these are absent in your own life? _____

_____

_____

_____

SHARE

Describe a situation in which you and a friend had a disagreement. How did you solve it? _____

_____

_____

_____

PRAYER

If any of Saul's attitudes are yours, confess them and seek forgiveness. If you are harboring any bitterness or resentment in your heart, confess it now. Seek God's forgiveness. Pray for courage to go to a friend and make peace. If someone doesn't love you, ask God to help that person.

CARE

If you have told a friend that you forgive her, do something for her this week to assure her that you were sincere.

PREPARE

Read Psalm 16. Make a list of assurances given to the believer whose God is the Lord.

11

THE BOUNDARY LINES OF FRIENDSHIP

"True friendship purifies and exalts. A friend may be a second conscience. The consciousness of what he expects from us may be a spur to high endeavor. The mere memory that he exists, though it be at a distance, may stifle unworthy thoughts and prevent unworthy actions." —James Stalker

Making friends can fall into two extremes. We can have too few friends, or we can have too many! In our desire to be loving, we attempt to know every neighbor in the block, every visitor at church. We suffer two consequences: we know many people superficially, but are not close to anyone; or the needs of our friends demand so much of us, we become physically and emotionally exhausted. We suffer "burnout."

Let's look at Psalm 16 for perspective. This psalm was written by David, a man who had many enemies and many friends. All his life he had to deal with people.

1. What was the source of David's decisions? (vv. 2, 7)

   the Lord was his security

2. What had the Lord assigned to David? (v. 5) _____

   spiritual inheritance

Note: The word *portion* refers to the choice parts of the sacrificial animal that were given to the priests and Levites. The Lord had given David His best gift, which was Himself. The word *cup* is a picture of the Lord's forgiveness through Jesus Christ. When we drink from this cup, we are saved from our sins.

David testifies that his "lot"—his position with God—is secure. This fact should give us much comfort and security. We do not have to act under pressure or in a frenzy. We do not have to overextend ourselves with relationships in order to earn extra points with God. We have God's love and forgiveness with us always.

3. God has set boundary lines for us. How does David describe these? (v. 6) *pleasant - not a burden*

4. In verses 7–11, David tells us when and where we can depend on the Lord's counsel.
   a. When? (vv. 7, 10) *night seasons; in the very end*
   b. Where? (v. 8) *before me, at my right hand*

God has set boundary lines—limits—for us, for our own good, and always under His guidance. We need to know our limits. God has set limits for other people. We cannot determine these.

5. a. What factors, applicable to everyone, affect the number of friends a person can have? _____

_____

_____

_____

b. What factors, applicable specifically to me, affect the number of friends that I can have? _____

_____

_____

_____

6. What resources do I have to help me choose my friends?
a. Psalm 16:7. _____

_____

b. 2 Timothy 3:16–17. _____

_____

c. John 14:16–17. _____

_____

d. Ephesians 5:22. _____

_____

e. Colossians 4:2. _____

_____

f. 1 Peter 5:1–2. _____

There are two emotional devices Satan can use to keep us from setting limits for our friendships. These are pride and guilt.

PRIDE

Here are some aspects of pride. Read them over privately and thoughtfully. Which ones may fit you?

- If I don't act in this situation, no one else will.
- I need many friends to make me feel important.
- I want to impress other people with my popularity.
- I enjoy having people depend on me.
- Influence and power over people make me feel good.

Romans 12:3 tells us how to regard ourselves.

GUILT

With guilt, we burden ourselves with everyone's problems. Rather than allowing each person to take responsibility for her own actions, we decide that somehow, her problems are our fault.

Divide into small groups and explore one of the following statements.

1. There is a difference between sharing our problems and dumping them all on someone else.

2. A friend does not have to respond to every phone call, every request for help, or every demand for a favor.

3. Our ever-ready assistance to a long-suffering friend can actually be a deterrent to her recovery.

SHARE

Certain types of neurotic and psychotic people, and particularly alcoholics, use guilt as a device to take the focus off their own weaknesses. if someone in the group has experienced such a problem with a friend, she may want to share her feelings.

As an alternative topic for discussion, return to your small group and explore another statement.

PRAYER

Ask God for discernment in making friends. If you are proud, seek humility. If you are feeling guilty, seek forgiveness. Claim the freedom from guilt given you by Christ's death on the cross.

CARE

For the next week, keep a diary of all the time you spend with your friends. Evaluate these experiences. Are you neglecting friends who really need your love and attention? Are you feeling exploited or suffocated by someone? Do you have friendships which are purely pleasurable on both sides?

PREPARE

Read Galatians 6:1–10. How do you interpret verse 2 in light of verse 5?

12

THE FRIENDLY CHURCH

"We have to give ourselves in honest friendship to people, if ever our relationship with them is to reach the point at which we are justified in choosing to talk to them about Christ, and can speak to them about their own spiritual needs without being either discourteous or offensive. If you wish to do personal evangelism, then—and I hope you do; you ought to—pray for the gift of friendship." —J. I. Packer

Friendship reaches its highest and sweetest form within the church, the body of Christ. Motivated by a desire to bring glory to God, church members care for each other, expressing love in thousands of ways.

In Galatians 6, Paul describes the roles of individuals within the body. Read the chapter now.

1. What are four guidelines for personal responsibility?

    v. 2. _____

    v. 3. _____

v. 4. _____

v. 5. _____

Note: The burden mentioned in verse 2 is a heavy weight pressing us down. The same word is used in John 19:17 to describe Jesus bearing the cross. The word *load* in verse 5 refers to a backpack carried by a porter or soldier on the march.

b. How do you think a person can obey verse 2 and verse 5? _____

_____

_____

_____

2. Do you see a conflict between verses 3 and 4? Are we supposed to be humble and proud at the same time?

_____

_____

_____

3. Verse 3 is connected to verse 2. We may think we are so perfect that we have no burdens for others to carry with us! From this self-deception comes the lack of regard for the burdens of others.
a. What do you see as your particular burdens? (These may be spiritual shortcomings, physical problems, emotional anxieties.) _____

_____

_____

_____

_____

b. Have you shared these with friends in your church? How have you been helped in the past? _____

_____

_____

_____

_____

4. Verse 4 directs us to bring our own work to the test: Is God pleased? We cannot apply our standard to the work of someone else. Our "pride" is based upon what God's grace has done in our life. What did Paul boast of? (v. 14)

_____

_____

5. a. Read 1 Corinthians 1:26–31 thoughtfully, then write how the Lord has changed you from "what you were when you were called" to what you are today. _____

_____

_____

_____

_____

b. What part have friends in your church played in your transformation? _____

_____

_____

_____

6. Some churches have a reputation for being friendly. Others are described as "cold." What do you consider to be the marks of a friendly church? _____

_____

_____

_____

_____

7. Make a list of things your church does to welcome visitors
   and make them feel at home. _____

_____

_____

_____

_____

8. How does your church encourage its people to build
   friendships? _____

_____

_____

_____

_____

SHARE

Discuss some ways your church can use friendship both to
evangelize those who do not know Christ, and to help those
who are Christians to become more like Him. Record these
suggestions. _____

_____

_____

_____

_____

_____

PRAYER

Thank God for His church and the special place it has in our lives. Thank God for Christian friends who share our burdens. Ask Him for sensitivity to see the burdens of others, and the strength to share them.

CARE

Share your suggestions for friendship with your minister or another officer in your church. Perhaps you and others in this Bible study can be the catalyst for a program of friendship evangelism or body life.

PREPARE

. . . To be a good friend!

HOW THE BODY OF CHRIST WORKS

LEADER'S GUIDE

INTRODUCTION

People come to Bible studies for all kinds of reasons. Learning what the Bible has to say may be the primary motivation, but sometimes that is not nearly as important as relieving boredom, being with other people, escaping routine and responsibility, reaffirming one's dogmatic position, or submitting to individual or group pressure. A woman whose husband forbade her to attend church on Sunday was able to combine Thursday morning Bible study with a weekly trip to the supermarket. For two hours she literally soaked up scriptural teaching and Christian fellowship, but always with the fear that her husband would find out and react violently. Another woman went primarily because she liked coffeecake.

"Friendship," as a topic, will draw people who want to know what the Bible has to say on the subject. It will also draw people who are looking for friends. Some of these seekers have a straightforward desire to make a friend or to be a better friend. Some, however, will come with complex emotional problems covering the gamut from diagnosed depression to rejection following a divorce. They desperately want someone to appreciate how intense their suffering is, to offer them love.

It is not the function of a workshop on friendship to offer professional counsel on emotional problems. Few leaders have the special training this work requires. The objective of this workshop is to encourage quality friendships both within and outside the group. The leader needs to move the group through the prescribed lessons at a pace which allows for individual response, but avoids digressions into an analysis of personal situations. When the leader becomes aware of a participant with acute needs, she should inform that person's pastor or, if she has none, tell her own pastor and let him decide what course of action is best. Since the majority of Bible studies are church-sponsored, the minister will probably know the person and can effectively relate the problem to the ministry of her church.

The very nature of a friendship workshop involves other responsibilities, however. The atmosphere should be warm and caring, with time for people to get to know each other. Throughout the book there are various exercises designed to stimulate friendships. Research of biblical passages is sometimes done in groups. Friendship is one subject we cannot learn through lectures!

As in all group Bible studies, the leader must have a deep sense of commitment. Lesson preparation and prayer are essential. There will be telephone conversations which seldom come when it is convenient. As the relationship between leader and students develops, some of the women will need to talk privately; the leader's work doesn't stop at the end of the lesson. Mind and spirit are active all week.

The enabling for this ministry comes from God's Holy Spirit. Paul's words to Timothy are meant for us, too: "For

God did not give us a spirit of timidity, but a spirit of power, of love, and of self-discipline" (2 Timothy 1:7). Ask God for these qualities as you prepare to lead this workshop, and throughout the series. He understands your needs and wants to help.

LEADER'S GUIDE

Lesson 1: What Is a Friend?

As each person arrives, have her write her name, address, and telephone number on a 3 x 5 card. You will compile this information into a list to be distributed next week to each one in the group. The cards are for your personal use, to make note of particular needs, and for prayer.

After the group is assembled, tell them something about yourself. Then ask each person to introduce herself by telling her name, address, and favorite television program. Distribute 3 x 5 cards and ask each person to write one thing about herself that no one else in the group knows. She is not to give her name. Collect the cards. This information will be revealed during lesson 9, when everyone will have an opportunity to guess who wrote the cards.

Ask the group to turn to lesson 1 in the workbook. Give time to answer the first question and hear any definitions that are volunteered. Share responses to questions 2 and 3.

4. Ask for suggestions. Incorporate these into the following five answers. Write out only the underlined portions.

(a) *Serves as a model for other relationships* —marriage, parent-child, employer-employee, neighbors. The practice we gain in loving and sharing with our friends prepares us for loving and sharing in other situations. The friendships of childhood are vital for building trust in our peers later in life.

(b) *Helps us to grow intellectually, emotionally, spiritually.* A friend wants us to be using our potential, exercising our gifts, and becoming more like Christ.

(c) *Helps us to know ourselves.* A friend praises and criticizes, encourages and restrains, acts as a second conscience. In intimate conversations with our friend—sharing dreams, seeking her opinion on ideas, responding to her counsel—we get a picture of what we are really like. Did you ever have a friend give you a cartoon or newspaper clipping that showed you something about yourself?

(d) *Provides an opportunity for us to practice love and unselfishness.* We can work out the many mandates in Scripture concerning relationships.

(e) *Cures loneliness*—the precursor to grief, feelings of abandonment, and depression.

5. As King Saul's son, Jonathan, was heir to the throne of Israel. He knew it was the Lord's will that David should be king instead. Not only did Jonathan not stand in David's way, he saved his life and offered himself as second in command.

6. (a) He rejoiced in David's success. He wasn't jealous. He gave a visible and public token of his friendship.

(b) He spoke well of David to his father. He pointed out his good characteristics and restored the relationship between his father and David.

(c) He offered encouragement to David when he was despondent. He was willing to do whatever he could to help. He gave wise counsel. He was truthful. He loved him as he loved himself.

(d) He endangered his own life to save David. He defended him. He grieved because David had been shamefully treated.

(e) He helped David to find strength in the Lord. He helped him to realize God's potential for his life. He made a covenant to prove his loyalty and commitment.

7. David and Jonathan recognized that each had separate roles to fill. Neither imposed on the other. David did not ask Jonathan to be disloyal to his father even though Saul was a potential threat. Jonathan did not expect David to do anything that would detract from his preparation to be king of Israel. Each man went his separate way, yet each performed an act of friendship when it was needed.

Share. Discussion questions can be used to pull together commetns made by the group during the study. If much interest is shown in the subject of child-rearing, for example, the leader can ask that discussion be saved until the end of the lesson. In this way the assigned material can be covered. It is important to keep your promise and have the discussion!

Prayer. Some people find it very difficult to pray spontaneously in front of others. Everyone can read from a card, however. Begin the prayer time with adoration and thanksgiving, asking each person to read what she has written. From this, move into confession and petition, allowing those who feel comfortable praying aloud to do so. Announce at the outset that you will be the last to pray, so it will be clear when the prayer time is finished.

Care. It is not necessary for anyone to say what she has chosen to pray about. Next week's meetings may be exciting as people report on what God has done!

Prepare. Encourage homework. The work can be done in the time it takes to watch one half-hour television show.

Lesson 2: The Perfect Friend

Welcome newcomers. Distribute the lists of names and addresses today, and have each person add new names to her sheet. Be sure everyone adds them in the same order, as this information will be used in the CARE activity this week.

Each newcomer should fill out a card telling something about herself that no one else knows. These cards should be placed with the others that are being held for lesson 9.

Review last week's lesson. What characteristics of friendship did Jonathan display toward David? The question may arise, "What did David do for Jonathan?" In 1 Samuel 4:4 and 9:1 we read the story of Mephibosheth. You can read it at this time, or assign it to be done at home.

Some in the group may be surprised to learn that Jesus has known us since the beginning of time. Supporting Scriptures are Isaiah 46:8–10; Jeremiah 1:5; and Ephesians 1:3–14.

Draw upon the reading of Psalm 139 done at home last week. We should be glad that God knows us so well. David said it was "wonderful."

Point out that we are "fearfully and wonderfully made." We are special, important to God. There is a tendency for Christians to degrade themselves. The seeds of depression lie in a feeling of worthlessness. Scripture does not teach this.

Even though we are sinners, we are still precious to God—so precious, He redeemed us by allowing His Son to die on our behalf. This is the ultimate proof of our value to our heavenly Father.

We cannot be selfless in our own power. There are many non-Christians doing "good" things, but they are not doing them to glorify God. Either they want to bring glory to themselves, or else they hope their good deeds will earn them a place in heaven. This is selfish benevolence, since the person is really looking out for herself.

This is an important lesson, even for the person who is already a Christian, since it lays the groundwork for knowing Jesus as a friend, and emulating Him through the power of the Holy Spirit. With depression so widespread among Christian women, this principle of self-worth needs to be reinforced. You will have to assess your particular group to decide where your emphasis should be this week.

Note: Even though the CARE activity seems mechanical, it is useful in motivating a person to send a card and then to be encouraged with subsequent appreciation. Sending cards and notes is a relatively easy way to be friendly, but many people have never learned to do so. Getting a card helps us to realize how much it means.

Lesson 3: Jesus Demonstrates Friendship

There is much Bible study in this chapter. To cover the material, assign verses to individuals. As answers are given, write them out on a chalkboard or easel pad so that those who write slowly can copy in their workbooks.

Share. Allow time for individual responses.

Prayer. This can be silent prayer, particularly if there are needs which are confidential.

Care. Ask for reactions to last week's assignment. Did anyone receive a note? Was it helpful? Encourage class members to write down specifically what they intend to do about their assignment this week, along with the date. Share with them, if you can, an occasion when you and a friend restored your relationship.

Prepare. Have some different Bible translations available to lend group members.

Lesson 4: The Traits of Friendship

It is always startling to discover God's priorities. If you have church leaders in your group, Paul's emphasis on being rather than doing may make them feel uncomfortable. Emphasize that it is not an either/or situation. We are not to sit around "feeling loving, but not working." Nor are we to perform our Christian tasks in an unloving manner. The goal is to use our gifts in a loving way.

6. (a) Recognize that love is not an option, but an act of obedience. It is the mark of a Christian. Our feelings of hatred or dislike may not turn into warm emotion overnight, but love toward others should be our goal.

(b) Imitate Christ. Jesus, who was thoroughly human as well as divine, gave us an example of how to love.

(c) Use the power of the Holy Spirit. True love is impossible in our own strength, but when we admit our weakness and ask God to enable us, He will show us how to love.

(d) Read Scripture and make it a part of your life. There is much encouragement and specific direction in God's Word.

(e) Become part of a church congregation. The body of Christ offers tremendous resources, a most important one being the love of other believers.

(f) Pray for a loving spirit. God will enable us to love when we never thought it possible.

Lesson 5: How Friendship Behaves

4. (a) Romans 14:7, 13: We are not "our own person," to do whatever we please. We are Christ's, and accountable to Him. While we are to be concerned for the way our friend expresses her Christian faith, we are not to be judgmental. Literally, "Let us no longer have the habit of criticizing one another." Secondly, we should not be an obstacle in the growth of another Christian. This has broad implications for the way we conduct ourselves, and for the counsel we offer our friends. See Matthew 7:1–2.

(b) 2 Corinthians 5:14–17: We regard no one from a worldly point of view. This rules out selfishness—looking out for No. 1. Nor are we to choose our friends on the basis of worldly values of class, money, prestige, and power. We see people from the perspective of Christ on the cross. We love mankind regardless of race or status.

(c) 1 Corinthians 6:18–20: Fleeing sexual immorality means taking ourselves away from people, places, and circumstances which promote it. The intimacy of friendship can lead us to harm our bodies if we proceed with a relationship in our own strength or without the counsel of other Christians. Our high regard for our bodies determines how we eat, sleep, work, exercise, have fun, relax, etc. So much of what we do is social that our choice of friends and what we do when we are with them is bound to be affected.

(d) 1 Thessalonians 5:10–11: Living with Christ should give us a positive attitude toward others. One of our greatest joys is encouraging people to use their gifts and talents. Building up may be as simple as saying "thank-you," or as complex as providing a scholarship so that a gifted young person can obtain more education. One characteristic of friendship is the mutual bringing out the best in the friend. This is different from the adoring "groupie" following the superstar, or the weaker personality acting as a servant for the stronger one. Each friend contributes to the other's growth and rejoices in her accomplishments.

Share. "My friends on the bowling team treat me better than my friends at church" is the kind of statement that causes us to ask if there really is a difference between Christian and non-Christian friends. Certainly there should be. Loving someone in Christ implies an ultimate purpose of bringing glory to God, and an immediate objective of doing what is best for that person's soul. To reach either goal requires prayer, sharing God's word, admonition, and encouragement where appropriate, humility, sensitivity, and the willingness to suffer for the friend's sake. If the friend is a Christian, we want to see her grow in grace. If she is not, we want to see her saved.

It must be admitted that non-Christian friends can love us deeply, even though their purpose for loving is not the same as ours. They also enrich our lives, often sharing work, recreation, and special interests. Scripture does not tell us to forsake all our old friends when we become Christians. A subsequent lesson will give some guidelines on this difficult issue.

Note: This is a good time to evaluate the workshop. Is everyone participating? Are two or three people dominating the group? Are you learning of deeper problems that need professional help? Keep adding notes about each woman on her 3 x 5 card. Can you put two people with common interests together so that they can develop a friendship? Are you praying for each of your students? Do you have a friend praying for you?

Lesson 6: The Value of a Good Friend—Part 1

A. Encouragement. The discussion of older women training younger women may bring to light strong feelings from both sides. Older women may not realize their responsibility or may fear rejection. Younger women may not appreciate the help when it is offered or given. The whole idea of respect for the wisdom and experience of an older person is foreign to our culture.

Point out that Paul is talking about teaching, as opposed to meddling or interfering. Teaching can take place in informal as well as formal situations. Much of it is simply "modeling"—being an example for the younger Christian.

B. Counsel. Not all friendships involve mutual counseling. This role is reserved for those special relationships of complete trust. Everyone needs at least one such friend who will wound us, if necessary. We must have receptive hearts when this happens. No defensiveness or rationalizations!

Prepare. The incident when Jesus refused to help his friends is related in Mark 10:35–40.

Lesson 7: The Value of a Good Friend—Part 2

A. How Jesus Helped. Q1. Healed the sick, taught Scripture, prayed, drove out demons, calmed the storm, raised the dead, trained others to be helpers, fed the hungry, shared burdens, paid His taxes, gave sight to the blind, provided wine at a wedding, washed the disciples' feet, comforted the bereaved.

We cannot perform miracles, but many of the things Jesus did, we can do also. We can follow His example and offer our services wherever they are needed.

How do we decide what kind of help a person needs? The best, but sometimes the hardest way, is to ask her! We can also ask people who know her well. We can make it a point to learn about particular situations that cause problems, such as raising a handicapped child, coping with a long-term disease, losing a loved one.

In the process of educating ourselves, we will learn some general ways to be helpful. The problem is that many people need help, but we do not know they are hurting.

B. Prayer. Assign each passage to be read aloud. You may want to record the answers in **Q2** on a blackboard or easel pad. They can then be copied in the workbooks.

Share. Discuss our reluctance to accept praise. Are we proud of our humility? Do we think it is unchristian to acknowledge our gifts and talents? A woman who baked fabulous coffeecakes always downgraded any compliments that came her way. Finally a friend said, "Connie, when you keep telling us that you don't bake very well, you make us feel like we don't have good judgment. We're so dumb we don't know a good coffeecake when we taste it!" She had never looked at it in that way before.

Prayer. Urge each woman in the group to find a prayer partner. Share what yours has meant to you.

Do you pray regularly for each member of your group?

Lesson 8: Choosing a Friend

The person newly come to Christ probably has a host of friends from her non-Christian lifestyle. She is our most zealous evangelist and has the most promising mission field. Yet she must resist those who would draw her back into their sinful practices. She needs help in handling this conflict.

Although young Christians may be more susceptible to friendships which are bad influences, no one is immune to them. During times of loss or of stress or out of fellowship with God, mature Christians can become involved with people who tempt them to sin. These people may be Christians themselves. A person who is trying to lose weight is not strengthened by a Christian friend who likes to eat all the time. Another friend may have the time and money to go shopping (interrupted by an expensive lunch), whereas this is poor stewardship for someone else.

Another problematic friend is the woman who needs constant attention. Sometimes she is an exploiter. Often she is a person who makes excessive demands that become so oppressive the recipient and her family suffer. This situation will be studied more fully in lesson 9.

There is much biblical material to cover in this lesson. Assign verses to individuals and let them give their answers for the whole group to record. Do not lecture through this chapter, but let God's Word speak for itself.

Next week you will use the cards filled out before the first lesson. Be sure everyone now attending the workshop has written down one thing about herself that no one else knows.

Lesson 9: Making Friends

During your pre-class get-together, display the cards telling something no one else knows about. Or, if you have typed them all on a sheet of paper, distribute copies and let the women guess who wrote each one. Use this game to demonstrate to the group that everyone has some unusual event in her past which merits knowing about. We should regard everyone we meet as a potential diamond mine. Sometimes we must dig to find the precious gem inside. It is also to be noted that each of us is worth knowing. We have a valuable contribution to make to the life of someone else.

Wherever the Lord leads us, we are surrounded by potential friends, though we may not realize it at the time. This fact is the springboard for the small group exercise about Arbutus Abercrombie. When the small groups reconvene, you may wish to list all the suggestions on a chalkboard or easel pad.

The study of Colossians 4:2–6, and sections **A, B,** and **C** should be worked out as a group.

The quotation from Henry Churchill King should spark a lot of discussion. His point about mothers will evoke strong feelings. Explain that one can be a good mother and still grow. Allow opinions to be expressed without taking a side yourself. In many churches, the issue of mothers being with their children has created conflict. There is the working mother who puts her children in preschool and the mother who doesn't believe in leaving her children with a baby sitter. Each side and all the variations in the middle need to appreciate the other points of view.

Moderate the discussion away from the issue of child-rearing practices and to a consideration of how women can help each other to grow even as they are mothers. If there are older women in the group, you may wish to interject the idea that mothers of teen-agers and of young adults need to be enriching their own lives so that they can be interesting to their children and relate to them as adult friends. Also include in the discussion those who do not have children. Do they feel the need to have children as friends?

Lesson 10: Saving a Friendship

1. Assign the passages in 1 Samuel to pairs. This should take just a few minutes. The answers are—

(a) Selfishness: Saul wantd David to meet his needs, to do what God should do.

(b) Possessiveness

(c) Jealousy

(d) Anger

(e) Avoidance, lack of communication

(f) Envy

(g) Hatred

Distinguish between jealousy and envy. Jealousy involves mental uneasiness from suspicion or fear of rivalry. Envy is jealousy carried to the point where you desire the other person's advantage and will take action to get it.

Going to another person with the intention of restoring a broken relationship is very difficult. After we have overcome our pride, we must be prepared to hear the other person say some things about us that are true but not complimentary. A third deterrent is our fear that our going will have no effect.

Point out that we are to be obedient—and go. The Holy Spirit changes the heart. We cannot do that. When we have done all we can, we can be at peace. Philippians 4:1–9, which refers to two women in the church who had trouble getting along, is helpful here.

Lesson 11: The Boundary Lines of Friendship

Work with the group in studying Psalm 16.

5. Answers might be: health, stage in life (retired people may have more time than working parents), location (apartment vs. ranch). Personal factors could be: "I have to care for my sick mother" or "My husband's job requries me to move often" or "I am very shy."

6. The answer to "resources" can become a trite list that everyone has heard before unless the group discusses ways that the resources can be used. We need to be specific in defining our problem and specific in seeking help. Our church is available to guide us as well as to provide encouragement and support.

By this time, the group should be comfortable enough to discuss "the problem nobody wants to talk about"—limiting friendships. Just the realization that it is a universal problem should be reassuring. Encourage honesty, with the promise of understanding how each person feels. Lead the group to see the importance of the body of Christ as the means to balanced friendships. If guilt is an acute burden, personal counseling is advisable. Often, just realizing that other people feel overburdened is sufficient therapy.

Some women in the group may be among those who do the burdening. They may have no idea what effect their behavior has on the other person. Make a clear distinction between a real cry for help and continual rehash of an old problem with no attempt made for its solution.

Lesson 12: The Friendly Church

The objective in this final lesson is a positive one, directing the student to appreciate the value of friendships in her church, and to consider how an atmosphere that promotes friendliness can be improved. No church is perfect, and some churches are friendlier than others; but all bodies of believers offer loving care in some measure. It is easy to be critical, forgetting the singular blessings that Christians have.

Some people have suffered traumatic, negative relationships within their particular churches and consequently blame all churches everywhere. They need to hear of positive experiences. Others have continued to be lonely in the midst of a large congregation. Perhaps an approach was made to include them in some activity, and they refused. This lesson points out the mutual responsibility of both the individual and the group.

The cartoon that follows this lesson is a helpful device for discussion. Do others in the workshop see burden-bearing in this way?

Be sure that the suggestions given in the SHARE time are recorded and given to the proper authority. If possible, arrange for someone in the group to take definite responsibility for seeing that the suggestions result in concrete action.

Distribute 3 x 5 cards and ask each woman to evaluate the workshop. What was most helpful? What was least helpful? What suggestions would she make to improve the study? Collect these and study them carefully for your own benefit. Then give them to the person in your church who arranges Bible studies, so that future workshops can be improved.

Members of the workshop may wish to conclude the study with a meal together. This can be simple or elaborate, depending on the needs and talents of the group. Refrain from planning this yourself; allow the students to arrange what pleases them.

The author would appreciate hearing from women who use this study. Correspondence may be addressed to her in care of Zondervan Publishing House, 1416 Lake Drive S.E., Grand Rapids, MI 49506.